We're from

Egypt

Victoria Parker

Welcome to Egypt!

Young Explorer

www.heinemann.co.uk/library
Visit our website to find out more information about **Heinemann Library** books.

To order:
☎ Phone 44 (0) 1865 888066
▤ Send a fax to 44 (0) 1865 314091
🖳 Visit the Heinemann Bookshop at www.heinemann.co.uk/library to browse our catalogue and order online.

First published in Great Britain by Heinemann Library, Halley Court, Jordan Hill, Oxford OX2 8EJ, part of Harcourt Education.
Heinemann is a registered trademark of Harcourt Education Ltd.

Editorial: Jilly Attwood and Kate Bellamy
Design: Ron Kamen and Celia Jones
Photographer: Roy Maconcachie/EASI-Images
Picture Research: Maria Joannou
Production: Séverine Ribierre

Originated by Ambassador Litho Ltd
Printed and bound in China by South China Printing Company

ISBN 978 0 431 11932 8 (hardback)
09 08 07 06 05
10 9 8 7 6 5 4 3 2 1
ISBN 978 0 431 11939 7 (paperback)
10 09 08
10 9 8 7 6 5 4 3

British Library Cataloguing in Publication Data

Parker, Victoria
We're From Egypt
962'.055

A full catalogue record for this book is available from the British Library.

Acknowledgements

Corbis/Royalty Free pp. **4a, 4b, 30a**; Getty Images/Photodiscp. **12**; Oxford Scientific Films p. **30c**; Roy Maconachie/EASI-Images pp. title page, **5, 6, 7a, 7b, 8a, 8b, 9, 10, 11, 13, 14a, 14b, 15a, 15b, 16, 17a, 17b, 18, 19a, 19b, 20a, 20b, 21a, 21b, 22a, 22b, 23, 24a, 24b, 25, 26a, 26b, 27a, 27b, 28a, 28b, 29, 30b**

Cover photograph of Karim, Heba, and their friend, reproduced with permission of Roy Maconachie/EASI-Images.

Many thanks to Karim, Ebtesam, Hamida and their families.

Every effort has been made to contact copyright holders of any material reproduced in this book. Any omissions will be rectified in subsequent printings if notice is given to the publishers.

Contents

Words appearing in the text in bold, **like this**, are explained in the Glossary.

 Find out more about Egypt at www.heinemannexplore.co.uk

Where is Egypt?

To learn about Egypt we meet three children who live there. Egypt is a big country in Africa. Most of the land is hot, dry **desert**.

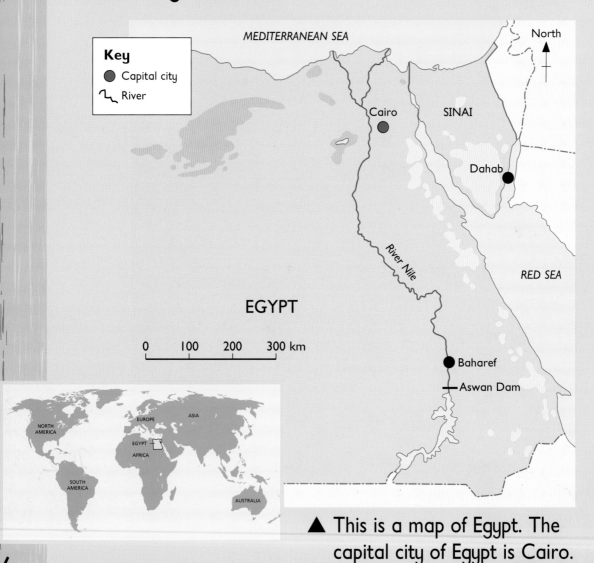

Key
- ● Capital city
- ∿ River

MEDITERRANEAN SEA

North

Cairo

SINAI

Dahab

River Nile

RED SEA

EGYPT

0   100   200   300 km

Baharef

Aswan Dam

NORTH AMERICA

EUROPE   ASIA

EGYPT

AFRICA

SOUTH AMERICA

AUSTRALIA

▲ This is a map of Egypt. The capital city of Egypt is Cairo.

The River Nile flows through Egypt. It runs from south to north. The land along the river is good for farming. This is where most Egyptians live.

▲ This Egyptian sailing boat is called a *felucca*.

Meet Karim

Karim is eight years old. He lives with his parents and his ten-year-old sister, Heba. Karim's father is a businessman. His mother is a teacher.

Karim

Heba

Karim's mother

Karim's father

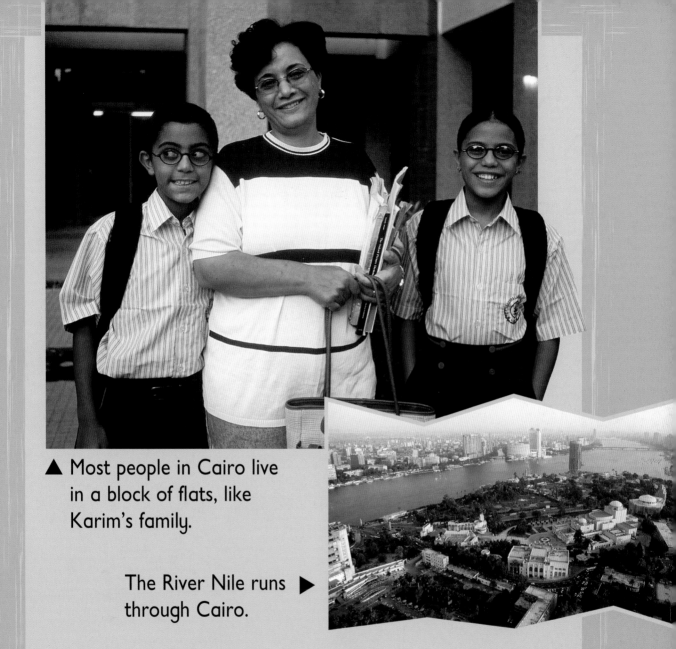

▲ Most people in Cairo live in a block of flats, like Karim's family.

The River Nile runs ▶ through Cairo.

Karim's family live in Egypt's capital city, Cairo. Their home is on the first floor of a tall block of flats.

Karim at school

Karim and Heba go to school every day except Friday and Saturday. School starts at eight in the morning. It finishes at four in the afternoon.

Karim's father drives ▶ them to school. Cairo has very busy roads.

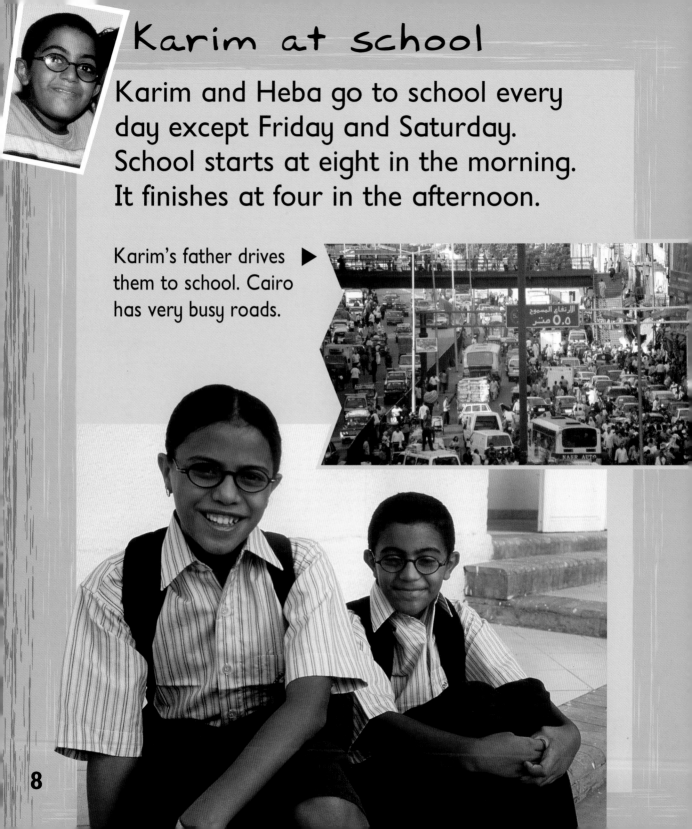

There are 25 boys and girls in Karim's class. Karim has lessons in English and Arabic. Arabic is Egypt's main language.

▼ The boys and girls line up outside school at the start of the day.

Karim at home

Karim enjoys Egyptian meals like bean stews, **kebabs** and salads. He eats his food by scooping it up in bits of flat bread. The bread is called *khoubz*.

Karim's grandmother

▲ Karim's grandmother lives nearby and comes round for dinner sometimes.

◀ Karim likes
inline skating.

After dinner and homework, Karim
and Heba play with their friends.
They play in front of their block of
flats. They like computer games and
painting too.

11

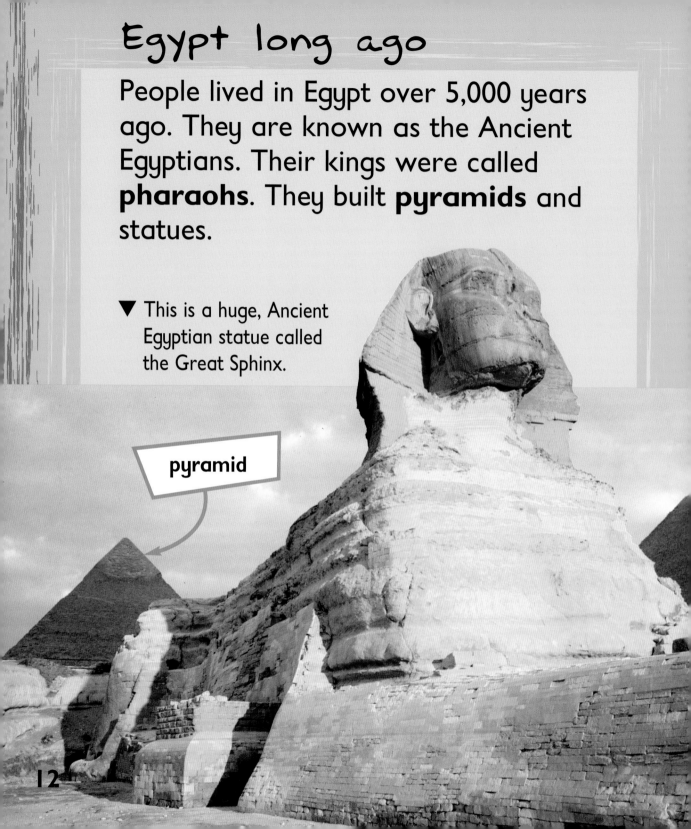

Egypt long ago

People lived in Egypt over 5,000 years ago. They are known as the Ancient Egyptians. Their kings were called **pharaohs**. They built **pyramids** and statues.

▼ This is a huge, Ancient Egyptian statue called the Great Sphinx.

pyramid

pyramid

Tourists come from all over the world to see the pyramids. These are where pharaohs were put when they died.

Meet Ebtesam

Ebtesam is six years old. She comes from Baharef. This is a village in south Egypt where people farm **dates**. She lives with her parents and her ten-year-old brother, Mohamed.

Ebtesam

Mohamed

Ebtesam's father

Ebtesam's mother

▲ Ebtesam's village is on the edge of the **desert**.

Ebtesam's uncles, aunts and cousins live in the same village. Everyone in the village has a house with a flat roof. They can dry dates in the sun on their roof.

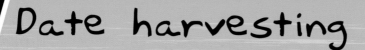

Date harvesting

Ebtesam's family do not have enough money to buy modern farming **equipment**. They do all the jobs on their farm using simple tools. It is very hard work.

▼ Mohamed climbs tall palm trees to pick the **dates**.

Ebtesam's family sell ▶
their dates at a
market like this one.

Ebtesam helps by carrying baskets full
of juicy dates. The family work
together to take the fruits off the
branches and to sort them.

17

Ebtesam's day

In the mornings, Ebtesam does her jobs on the farm. Her family plant vegetables to eat, as well as growing **dates** to make money. They keep chickens, too.

▲ One vegetable they grow is called *molokiyya*. It is a bit like spinach.

▲ Ebtesam's school has a yard for the children to play in.

Some children go to school for the morning. Ebtesam and her friends go to school in the afternoon. She has two hours of homework every day.

19

Ebtesam's home

Ebtesam's home has **electricity** but no running water. Ebtesam gets all the water for the family from the village pump.

◀ Getting water from the pump is hard work!

Ebtesam's family sit on the floor to
eat. Sometimes they cook on a small
heater in the kitchen. Other times,
they cook over an outside fire.

Weather and water

It does not rain very often in Egypt. Farmers have to use water from the River Nile to help their crops grow.

Sometimes farmers ▶ use donkeys to help move water onto their fields.

About 50 years ago, a huge **dam** was built on the River Nile at Aswan. The dam collects water from the river. People can use it to water their crops.

▲ The dam stops the river flowing as quickly, and makes a lake behind it.

Meet Hamida

Hamida is six years old. She lives with her parents and sister, Sara. They have a house in a town called Dahab, in the Sinai **Desert**.

Hamida's father

Hamida's mother

Sara

Hamida

◀ Dahab is a long way from the River Nile.

Hamida's family are **Bedouin** people. Bedouins **traditionally** live in tents. Hamida's family often go to stay at a Bedouin camp in the desert mountains.

▼ Hamida's family have lots of friends at the mountain camp.

Hamida helps out

Hamida does not go to school.
She has lots of jobs to do at home.
She is in charge of looking after her
family's herd of goats.

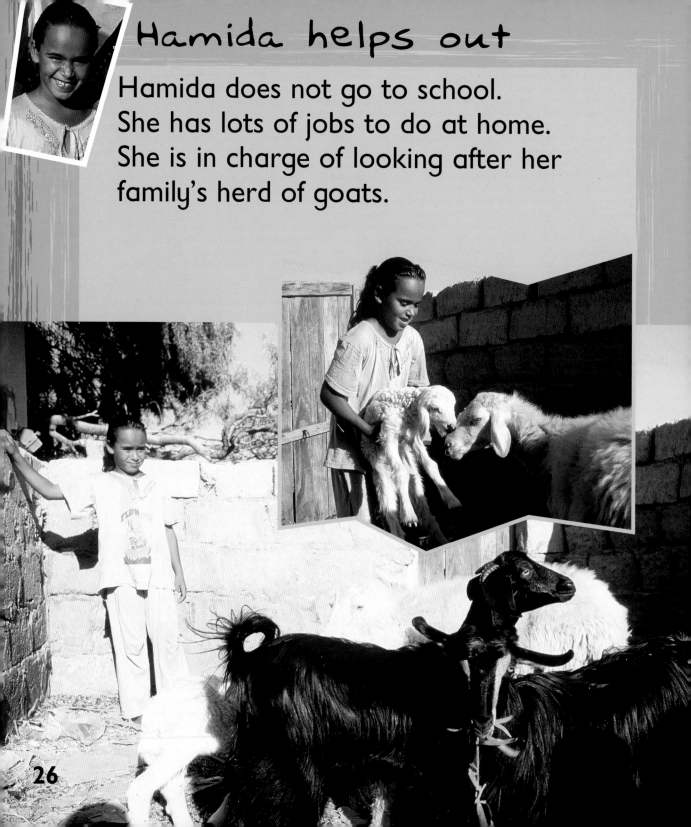

Hamida also helps her parents with the cooking. Hamida's father makes some very tasty bread!

The bread is ▶ baked and eaten with vegetables.

Life in the desert

Many tourists visit the Sinai for a holiday. They often pay to visit the **Bedouin** camp. Hamida and her mother make bracelets and crafts to sell.

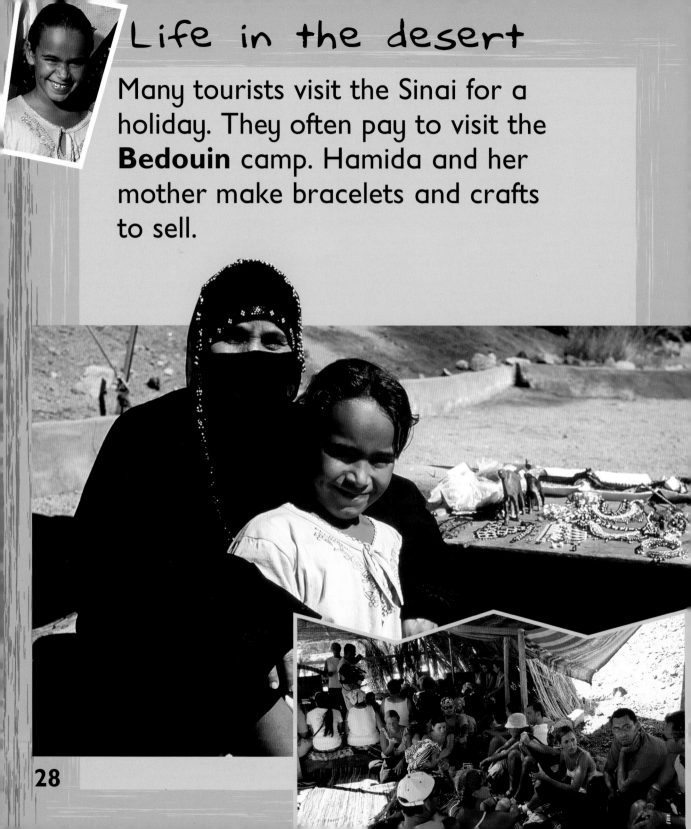

▼ Many Bedouins keep camels. Camels are good at walking on desert sand.

Hamida's father earns money by taking the tourists on trips in the **desert**. Bedouins know all about desert animals and plants, and where to find water.

Egyptian fact file

Flag

Capital city

Cairo

Money

Pounds and piastres

Religion
• Most people in Egypt are Muslims. There are some Christians too.

Language
• The main language of Egypt is Arabic. Many people also speak English, and some speak French.

Try speaking Egyptian Arabic!

salaam aleikum....................hello

izzayak...................................how are you?

shukran..................................thank you

 Find out more about Egypt at www.heinemannexplore.co.uk

Glossary

Bedouin an old tribe (group of people) who live in tents in the desert. They often move around rather than living in one place.

dam wall built across a river to make a huge lake behind it

dates fruit that grows on palm trees

desert very hot, dry area of land that has almost no rain and very few plants

electricity power used for heating, lighting, and working equipment

equipment tools and machines that help you do a job

kebabs type of grilled sausage or meat

pharaoh king who ruled Ancient Egypt

pyramid huge stone building in the desert, made as a tomb for pharaohs

tradition something that has been going for a very long time without changing

More books to read

Continents: Africa, Leila Foster and Mary Fox (Heinemann Library, 2002)

Habitat Explorer: Desert Explorer, Greg Pyers (Raintree, 2004)

Mummies, Pyramids and Pharaohs, Gail Gibbons (Little Brown, 2004)

Index